Creature Features

Exploring Animal Characteristics

Lisa Rao

Contents

Rigby
A Harcourt Achieve Imprint

www.Rigby.com
1-800-531-5015

Introduction

Have you ever wondered what the difference is between a frog and a toad, or an alligator and a crocodile? We all know there are millions of amphibians, reptiles, birds, insects, and mammals roaming the planet, but do you know how they were born or where they live? How big are they? What do they eat? How do they stay safe? Animals have many differences that allow scientists to classify, or sort, them into groups. Whether an animal has feathers or fur, lives in the water or on land, it still shares certain **characteristics** in common with other animals.

All animals, for example, have a life cycle. A life cycle includes being born, growing into an adult, **reproducing,** and dying. Look at the life cycle of an alligator on the next page. It shows the alligator at birth, growing into adulthood, and as an adult. The adult alligator will reproduce and start the cycle over again.

As animals move through their life cycles, they must also eat and stay safe. How they do these things depends on their characteristics.

Let's look at some groups of animals and explore some of the key characteristics all of the members of that group share. We will also explore the **unique** characteristics of some particular members in how they live, eat, and stay safe.

Alligator Life Cycle

eggs in nest

young alligator

adult alligator

3

Amphibians

Amphibians are **cold-blooded** creatures that lead double lives. Sound interesting? Amphibians certainly are!

Amphibians have backbones; therefore, they are called *vertebrates.* They also have smooth skin, and they are cold-blooded. This means that their bodies are the same temperature as the air or water around them.

Now about their double life—most amphibians hatch in the water and live there as they grow. As adults, they live on land. However, when it is time to lay their eggs, they return to the water.

Amphibians are born with gills that help them breathe underwater, just like fish. Later, some of them develop lungs that help them breathe outside of the water.

There are three groups of amphibians: frogs and toads, salamanders, and caecilians. Caecilians are blind, wormlike animals that live underground. They look like worms or small snakes. Salamanders live near streams and in moist forest areas, like wet logs or under leaves. Frogs live near lakes and ponds. Let's get to know these animals a little better!

Caecilians, salamanders, and frogs all live near the water.

Frogs and Toads

Frogs and toads make up the largest group of amphibians on the planet, with more than 4,000 **species**.

● How are frogs and toads born and how do they grow?

Like all amphibians, frogs and toads lay their eggs in the water. Some frogs lay only a few eggs, while others lay as many as 30,000 eggs at a time.

When baby frogs and toads hatch, they are called tadpoles or polliwogs. Tadpoles start out looking more like fish than frogs because they don't have legs and they breathe through gills. They also have long tails. As tadpoles mature, their tails become part of their bodies. They also grow hind legs, a pair of front legs, and their gills change into lungs.

Facts About Tadpoles

- Tadpoles swim by wriggling their bodies from left to right.
- Tadpoles eat algae.
- Some tadpoles live in schools, like fish, and can dart quickly in any direction.

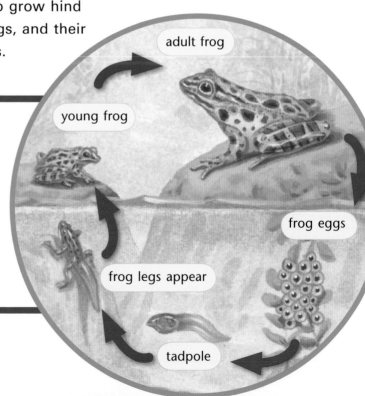

adult frog

young frog

frog eggs

frog legs appear

tadpole

● What do frogs and toads eat?

Luckily for us, frogs and toads eat insects, especially ones that we consider pests, such as mosquitoes and flies. Most frogs absorb all of their water through their skin. Many have a special drink-patches on their stomachs.

They catch their food with their long, sticky tongues that are attached to the front of their mouth instead of the back, like in humans. The placement of the tongue allows it to flip out and back faster than you can wink an eye!

● How are frogs and toads different?

Frogs and toads are very much alike; in fact, all toads are part of the frog group. The biggest difference between the two, however, is that most frogs spend much of their adult lives in water, while adult toads live on land.

There are also physical differences. Frogs are thin, have smooth, moist skin, and usually have teeth on their upper jaws. Toads are chubby, have rough, dry skin, and have no teeth. Frogs also have long back legs for leaping, while toads have short, stubby back legs for hopping.

Now that you know the difference, which is the frog and which is the toad?

Salamanders

The word *salamander* means "something that can withstand fire," but these creatures prefer to stay moist and cool. Salamanders are smaller amphibians with over 300 different species, including a wide variety of newts, which are salamanders that spend part of their lives on land.

● What do salamanders look like?

Salamanders look like lizards, except they don't have scales. Like most amphibians, they have gills when they are born, and as they mature, they develop lungs. Most salamanders have four toes on their front feet and five toes on their hind feet. Their skin, which they shed as they outgrow it, is moist and usually smooth. Once it's shed, salamanders will eat their old skin! They are quiet, **nocturnal** animals. They go out at night in search of insects, worms, snails, and small fish to eat.

Compare the World's Largest and Smallest Salamanders

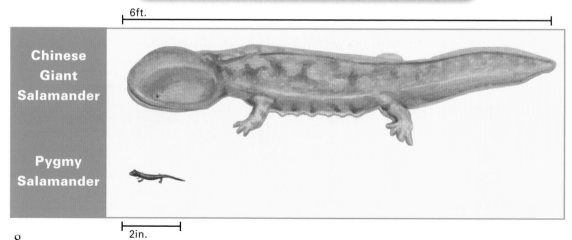

6ft.

Chinese
Giant
Salamander

Pygmy
Salamander

2in.

Salamanders come in lots of different colors.

● Where do salamanders live?

Some adult salamanders live in ponds and streams. Others live in damp places that are cool and dark, such as under stones or in hollow logs found in a shady woods. They never stray far from water because, if they can't keep their skins moist, they will die.

● How do salamanders protect themselves?

All salamanders have poison in their skin that can hurt or even kill a **predator**. Many have bright colors and patterns on their skin to let snakes and other animals know they are **toxic**. If a snake tries to eat a California slender salamander, for example, the poison glues the mouth of the snake closed!

Salamanders are also able to grow new limbs. This is called *regeneration*. If, during a fight with a snake or other predator, the salamander were to have a leg or its tail bitten off, it would simply grow a new one! The limb grows right out of the old stump, good as new.

9

Caecilians

At first glance, this amphibian looks like a big worm—or is it a snake? It is long, slender, and without legs. More often than not, it's almost impossible to tell the front end from the back. It spends almost all of its life burrowing underground, and its eyes don't see much beyond light and dark. So what is it? This creature is a caecilian (suh-SILL-yun).

The caecilian gets its name from the Latin word *caecus,* which means blind. It has a layer of skin over its eyes to protect it as it burrows underground.

● Where do caecilians live?

Caecilians are found in damp parts of the world, mostly in the Southern Hemisphere, in places like Central Africa, South America, and Southeast Asia. They are rarely seen because they remain underground. Their hard, pointy skulls help them dig through the dirt. They spend their entire lives underground, where it's dark and moist.

● What do caecilians eat?

Despite their soft appearance, caecilians have needle-sharp teeth that allow them to feed on termites, grub worms, and other bugs. They don't hunt for their food; they wait for their dinner to wander nearby, then they snatch it up with their needle teeth.

Reptiles

What is that scaly creature creeping up on a rock to bathe in the sun? Chances are, it is a reptile. After all, the word *reptile* does mean "to creep"!

Reptiles are cold-blooded creatures that are different from amphibians in that they breathe using lungs. Plus, many of them spend most of their time on land. Like amphibians, reptiles lay eggs, but the eggs are typically covered with a thick, leathery shell. The eggs are also often laid on land.

There are about 6,800 reptile species found on every continent except Antarctica. The main groups of reptiles living today are snakes and lizards, turtles, alligators and crocodiles, and tuataras.

Dinosaurs were reptiles, too. The earliest known reptile is *Hylonomus lyelli,* which lived 315 million years ago. It was almost 8 in. long, including its tail, and probably looked like the lizards we see today. It had small, sharp teeth and probably ate millipedes and other early insects.

Reptiles are known for their scaly skin and cold-blooded nature.

Snakes

Snakes are long, slender, limbless reptiles with scaly skin and lidless eyes. There are over 2,000 species of snakes throughout the world. They can be found in the desert, in the sea, deep underground, and high in the trees.

● How do snakes find food?

Snakes have noses, but most snakes actually smell for food with their tongues! They stick out their forked tongues to gather odor particles in the air. When the tongue goes back in, it is placed into two holes in the roof of the snake's mouth, where the odor is smelled.

The pit viper has a hole between its eyes that is sensitive to heat. This allows it to locate its prey by heat, rather than sight. It can find food in total darkness!

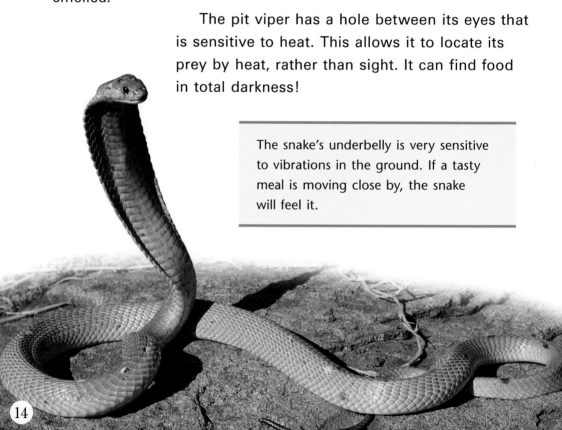

The snake's underbelly is very sensitive to vibrations in the ground. If a tasty meal is moving close by, the snake will feel it.

● Why do snakes shed their skin?

Snakes must shed their skin about once a month because it is made of scales that don't stretch and grow with the snake, like human skin does. The whole process takes about one or two weeks. The snake starts by loosening the skin around its nose and mouth, then it glides over a rock or other surface to help pull the old skin off. The shed skin is often in one piece that is hollow like a sleeve of a shirt or an empty sock.

Slithering Snakes

- At only 4 in. long, the dwarf blind snake is the smallest snake in the world.
- The reticulated python is the longest snake at lengths up to 33 ft. long.
- The black mamba is the fastest land snake. It can travel short distances at 10 to 12 mph.

In addition to being fast, the black mamba is also deadly. Before it strikes, it will look directly into the eyes of its prey.

15

Lizards

The lizard makes up the largest group of reptiles. These reptiles can be found everywhere on Earth except in the freezing areas of Antarctica, the Arctic, and the northern part of North America.

● How are lizards born?

Most lizards dig a hole in which they lay their tough, leathery eggs. Iguanas, for example, may lay 50 or more eggs in a hole at one time. The eggs take about 8–10 weeks to hatch and only 3–10 babies live to adulthood in the wild.

After laying, most lizards do not protect their eggs or raise their young. Iguanas, however, have an interesting way of trying to protect their young. They dig fake holes to confuse predators that feed on iguana eggs.

House geckos have toe pads to help them climb vertically. They are gentle insect eaters and are commonly seen around homes in warm regions such as Texas and the Southwest.

What do lizards eat?

Most lizards eat insects and rodents, while some eat seeds. A few only eat vegetables.

How do lizards protect themselves?

Many lizards can run quickly and have sharp spines along their heads and backs. Some, like the chameleon lizard, can hide from other animals using **camouflage**. If an animal tries to grab a lizard by the tail, they are out of luck because when a lizard's tail is touched, it falls off. A new tail grows in its place.

Chameleons are unique animals. They can change color, move their eyes in different directions, and have very long, sticky tongues to catch their prey. They can also use their tails to hold tight to branches.

Skinks move through sand more like snakes than lizards. Young bluetail mole skinks of Florida have blue tails that turn a pink color as they mature.

Alligators

Alligators are the large, **carnivorous** reptiles that spend time both in water and on land. Their bodies are slightly rounded with thick arms and legs. They have wide heads and long tails that measure half the length of their bodies. Alligators are only found in two countries on the planet, the United States and China. They prefer to live in swamps, marshes, and lakes where it's damp and cool.

● How are alligators born?

Alligators would crush their eggs if they sat on them, so females build 3-foot tall by 6-foot wide nests of mud, leaves, and twigs in which they lay up to 50 eggs.

Believe it or not, how hot or cold the nest is determines whether baby alligators will be male or female. If the eggs **incubate** at temperatures over 93° Fahrenheit, the **embryos** develop as a male. Incubation below 86° F results in a female embryo, and between 87° and 92° F, either male or female embryos can be produced.

The eggs hatch in 2 months, producing hatchlings about 6 in. long. Alligators are nurturing reptiles and protect their hatchlings for a year.

Newborn alligator hatchlings are about 6 in. long.

● What do alligators eat?

Alligators are nocturnal eaters, which means that they eat at night. Younger alligators eat insects, shrimp, snails, small fish, tadpoles, and frogs. Adult alligators eat fish, birds, turtles, other reptiles, and mammals. Alligators use their teeth to catch prey, and then they swallow it whole.

● What is the difference between an alligator and a crocodile?

The easiest way to tell the difference between an alligator and a crocodile is to look at their faces. The crocodile's face is long and pointy, while the alligator has a short, wide face. You can see a crocodile's teeth even when its mouth is closed. In an alligator, the teeth are hidden.

All About Alligators

- The american alligator is the largest reptile in North America.
- Before 1960, the alligator almost became extinct.
- An alligator has no vocal chords. So in order to make noise, it sucks air into its lungs and blows, which makes a roaring sound.

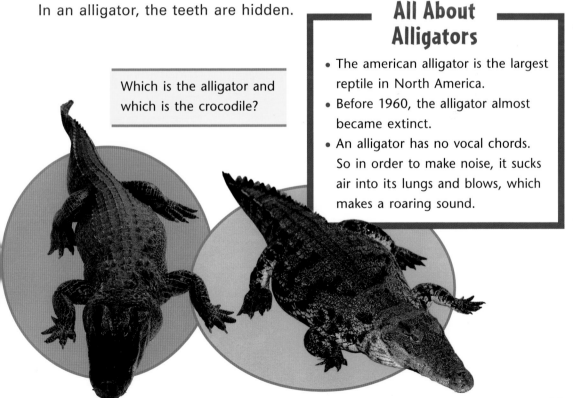

Which is the alligator and which is the crocodile?

Turtles

When you think of reptiles, you're probably not thinking cute and cuddly. But actually, the turtle is a popular household pet. Well, at least the small ones are. There are many types of turtles that you can't squeeze into your aquarium, unless it can hold a 1,300 lb. sea turtle!

In England, if a turtle lives in a lake or pond, it is called a terrapin. If it lives on land, it is called a tortoise.

● How are turtles born?

All turtles hatch their young in eggs, but no other turtle does it quite like the leatherback turtle. The leatherback is a type of sea turtle, and it lives its whole life out at sea. In fact, once the male leatherback hatches and leaves the beach, it will never set food on land again. The female leatherback only returns to land every 3 to 4 years, and always to the exact same beach where she herself was hatched. The female digs a nest, lays between 60 and 170 golf ball-sized eggs, and then returns to the ocean. The baby leatherbacks hatch 55 to 65 days later, and then they also head out to spend their lives in the sea.

● How do turtles protect themselves?

The turtle is best known for its protective shell. This shell is made out of bony material that is attached to the turtle's body, which means that the turtle cannot crawl out of its shell, as crabs and snails do. For protection, the turtle will pull its head and legs into its shell, folding them close to its body. While hiding like this, it is difficult for a predator to crush the turtle in its jaws.

Mud turtles get their name from the way they hibernate in winter—they bury themselves in the mud of ponds and streams.

21

Tuataras

Tuataras (too-uh-TAHR-uh) are ancient reptiles that have roamed the planet since the time of the dinosaurs—that's almost 200 million years! Their closest relatives died long ago, but tuataras somehow survived on islands near New Zealand.

● What do Tuataras look like?

Tuataras look like big-headed lizards, but they are not considered lizards. They have spines on their backs that can fan out and protect them from danger. They do everything slowly, even breathing! They breathe only once an hour.

Tuataras live on islands near New Zealand, and there are laws that protect them from being taken off the island.

As Old as a Dinosaur

- *Tuatara* is a Maori word that means "peaks on the back."
- The tuatara is sometimes called a "living fossil."
- A tuatara is born with a third eye that becomes covered with scales after four to six months.

● What is the lifespan of Tuataras?

Tuataras lay 6–10 eggs at a time and bury them in a warm nesting hole. Babies hatch in 11–16 months and continue to grow until they are about 35 years old. Most tuataras live to be 60 years old but can live to be over 100!

● What do Tuataras eat?

Tuataras mostly eat insects, lizards, seabird eggs, and chicks.

Birds

Any animal with feathers and wings is considered a bird, and there are about 8,000–10,000 species of these warm-blooded vertebrates worldwide.

Birds are the only living animals with bones that can fly, except for bats, which are mammals. However, not all birds fly. The ostrich, cassowary, rhea, emu, moa, kiwi, and penguin are among those birds that are grounded for life.

Birds come in a variety of sizes, too. The smallest bird, the hummingbird, is just 2.5 in. long and weighs less than one-tenth of an ounce. The largest bird, the ostrich, can be up to 8 ft. tall and weigh about 300 lbs.

The ostrich, a native bird of the African savanna, is not only the largest bird, it also lays the biggest eggs, weighing up to four lbs. each. The hummingbird, on the other hand, lays two eggs the size of green peas.

● How do birds fly?

A bird's body is light and has built-in pockets of air for flying. Most of their bones are hollow, which means that birds don't have to lift much weight into the air. A bird also has strong muscles for flapping its wings.

The inner part of a bird's wing lifts the bird up into the air like an airplane. The outer part of the wing acts like a propeller. Its long feathers pull on the air and move the bird forward.

Hummingbirds can beat their wings up to 80 times per second and can fly around 27 mph. Penguins, however, use their wings for swimming, not flying.

Passerines

Passerines, also known as songbirds or perching birds, are the largest group of birds on the planet. With about 5,400 species, passerines are more **diverse** than rodents, which are the largest group of mammals.

● How are passerines born?

Most passerines build nests in a variety of shapes and places. Unlike other birds, passerines lay colored or speckled eggs that range from the blue of a robin's egg to the green of a crow's egg. Some non-passerine birds, such as some types of cuckoos, often lay colored eggs as well, just so they can leave them in passerine nests. The passerine then raises the cuckoo as her own, sometimes to the harm of the other chicks.

How do passerines sing?

Passerines often sing songs to recognize or to be recognized by other birds of the same species. The birds' song can be a warning, or a greeting. Most often, however, male birds sing to attract female mates.

Passerines have a special part of their throats that works much like the vocal cords of mammals. When this part vibrates, it can produce several sounds at once. In some species, like parrots, this part allows the bird to copy human speech.

How do passerines perch?

Passerines are also known as perching birds because they are able to grasp and balance on small branches, railings, and even wire. They are able to do this because their feet have three toes pointing forward and one toe pointing backward. This arrangement lets them lock their toes around their perch so they don't fall off.

Migratory Birds

Migratory birds are birds that fly to other regions in the winter to search for food and warmer weather. There are many migratory species of birds, such as geese, ducks, swallows, and swans. The longest known migration of a bird is that of the Arctic tern, which migrates from the Arctic to Antarctica and back each year. The routes that certain bird species take to migrate are called *flyways*.

One interesting kind of migratory bird is the trumpeter swan, a large water bird that lives in North America. It gets its name from its call, which sounds like a trumpet. Let's take a closer look at the trumpeter swan to learn more about migratory birds.

Waterproof birds? The feathers of swans, ducks, and geese not only keep them warm through the winter, they also keep them dry. Their feathers are coated with natural oils that help water to slide off, not soak into, their bodies.

What do trumpeter swans look like?

Trumpeters are long-necked white birds with a flat bill. They have black legs, black webbed feet, and thick feathers to protect them from cold weather. The wingspan of these birds is over 7 ft., and they are about 4 ft. tall.

What do trumpeter swans eat?

Young swans, or cygnets, eat lots of bugs and small invertebrates from the water's surface, while adult trumpeter swans eat mostly water plants like cattails and pondweeds. Their tails and legs go up in the air as their long necks reach deep under the water to eat these plants and their roots.

What are trumpeter swans' nests like?

Trumpeter swans build large nests made of grass, roots, and reeds and are lined with soft feathers called swan down. These nests are often built on top of a muskrat's den. Females lay 5–6 white eggs in each clutch (a set of eggs laid at one time) and defend their nests from any threat.

Trumpeter Swan Facts

- Trumpeter swans live about 12 years in the wild and about 35 years in captivity.
- Trumpeters almost went extinct 100 years ago. They now are protected by law and are growing in number.

Penguins

All 17 species of penguins live in the Southern Hemisphere. They are flightless birds and excellent swimmers. They can't breathe underwater, but they can hold their breath for several minutes at a time. While swimming, they will often leap high into the air to get a gulp of air before diving back down for fish.

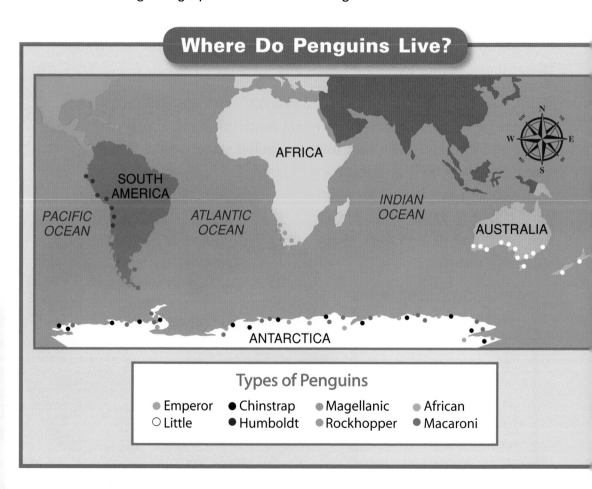

Where Do Penguins Live?

AFRICA

SOUTH AMERICA

INDIAN OCEAN

PACIFIC OCEAN

ATLANTIC OCEAN

AUSTRALIA

ANTARCTICA

Types of Penguins

- Emperor
- Little
- Chinstrap
- Humboldt
- Magellanic
- Rockhopper
- African
- Macaroni

What do penguins eat?

Penguins love seafood! They eat lobster, crabs, shrimp, and squid. Their bills have a hook at the end for grabbing their dinner. Stiff, hair-like material on their tongues called *bristles* keep slippery sea critters from getting away.

How do penguins stay warm in cold places?

Penguins have a thick layer of fat called blubber that keeps their body heat from escaping. Their bodies are covered with two layers of warm feathers: fluffy, down feathers and an outer layer of feathers. Together with the oil from a special penguin gland, these feathers are waterproof and windproof.

Emperor penguins in Antarctica will huddle close together to keep warm. These huge groups of penguins stand closely-packed, shoulder to shoulder, so they can share body heat. To keep their eggs from touching the ice and freezing, they balance them on their feet.

Penguin Facts

- Rockhopper penguins build their nests on steep, rocky areas. To get there, they hold both feet together and bounce from ledge to ledge.
- Magellanic penguins dig burrows under the ground to form huge "cities."
- Penguins bond with their mates by touching necks and slapping each other on the back with their flippers, and they'll also call to each other and learn to recognize each other's voices.

A penguin's colors help to disguise it from predators. An orca whale looking up in the water could mistake a penguin's white belly for the white surface of the water.

Birds use their keen eyesight to find food. Eagles have eyesight that's five to six times sharper than human eyesight and can spot even small prey from a mile away.

Birds of Prey

The cry of a powerful hawk sounds from above. In a flash a set of sharp claws are sprung, and the bird dives out of the sky to snatch up a small animal for its meal. The hawk then carries the creature off to eat in private. This winged hunter is a bird of **prey**, a type of bird that is definitely *not* into birdseed.

● How do birds of prey hunt?

Hawks, eagles, falcons, and owls all have an appetite for meat. They especially like mice, rats, rabbits, squirrels, and other small birds. Predator birds have very sharp eyes to see these small animals while flying high up in the sky. In fact, they can see five to six times better than humans see.

A predator bird's body is perfectly designed for the hunt. Their strong feet and sharp claws, or talons, snatch their prey off the ground and clutch it tight as the bird flies back up into the sky. They also have sharp, hooked beaks that are perfect for tearing into their food.

● How do birds of prey fly?

Birds of prey have different shaped wings depending on how they catch their food. For example, eagles soar high above the ground, watching out for a possible kill. They glide, rather than repeatedly flapping their wings, and so the feathers at the end of their broad wings are wide and fan out. On the other hand, the wings of a hawk are short and rounded. They fly quickly, zooming around trees and bushes as they hunt.

barbs

primary feathers

shaft

vanes

secondary feathers

quill

A bird's flight feathers are called *primary* and *secondary feathers*. They give a bird its shape, help lift it into the air, and keep it flying. Feathers are light and flexible but very strong. A hollow shaft runs down the center of the feather, and the shaft's side branches are called *vanes*. Each vane has a number of sections called *barbs* that are hooked together like a knitted scarf. The base of the feather is called a *quill*. If a bird damages its secondary feathers, it loses some control but still can fly. A bird cannot fly without its ten biggest primary feathers.

Insects

Buzzing, stinging, creeping, and crawling . . . these creatures are everywhere! Insects are the most diverse group of animals on Earth. There are about 925,000 different species. That's more than all other animal groups combined! Insects can also be found nearly everywhere, but only a small number of insect species are able to live in the ocean.

Spiders are often called insects, but that is not the case. Spiders are arachnids with eight legs. Insects have:

- a hard outer covering instead of a backbone,
- three main body parts (head, thorax, and abdomen),
- two antennae,
- six legs, and
- two pairs of wings.

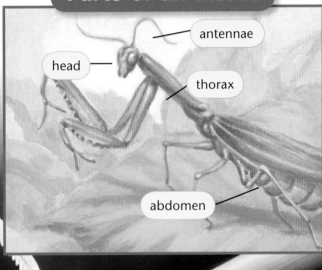

Parts of an Insect

antennae

head

thorax

abdomen

About one million different species of insects have been identified so far, and more are being discovered all the time.

Butterflies and Moths

Butterflies and moths are flying insects that are very closely related, especially in their life cycle. They both lay eggs that grow into caterpillars in the first two stages of their life cycles. These caterpillars then go through different processes to become butterflies or moths. There are 15,000–18,000 species of butterflies and 100–150 species of moths found worldwide.

● How do caterpillars turn into butterflies?

Butterflies go through **metamorphosis**, which means "change of form." First, the butterfly's egg grows into a caterpillar that eats many plant leaves. The caterpillar, now fairly large, then attaches itself to a twig and grows a hard skin, or pupa. This pupa is called a *chrysalis*. Weeks, or sometimes months later, the chrysalis splits open. A butterfly with tiny, damp wings appears. The butterfly hangs onto a twig until its wings dry out, and then it flies away.

The Butterfly Life Cycle

larva (caterpillar)

egg

butterfly

pupa (chrysalis)

● How do caterpillars turn into moths?

When a moth egg chews its way out of its egg, it grows into a larva, a multi-legged worm-like creature. The larva eats constantly, and once the larva is very large, it attaches itself to a tree, sheds its skin, and spins a hard, protective cocoon around itself. This cocoon is made of strong silk, which the larva makes in its body. The larva rests inside its cocoon and slowly changes into a moth. Then the moth comes out of its covering and flies away.

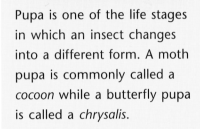

Pupa is one of the life stages in which an insect changes into a different form. A moth pupa is commonly called a *cocoon* while a butterfly pupa is called a *chrysalis*.

● What's the difference between a moth and a butterfly?

A moth usually flies at night while a butterfly flies during the day. The body of a moth is thick and hairy, while the body of a butterfly is thin and not at all hairy. The feelers of a butterfly are slender and have little knobs at the ends, while the moth's feelers don't have these knobs and are often quite fuzzy. A butterfly also often has brighter colors on its wings.

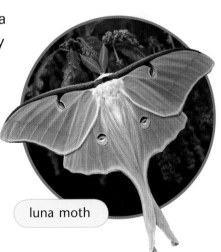

luna moth

Ants

Ants are small, social insects that live with other ants in an organized colony. There are thousands of species of ants that vary in size, color, and way of life. Some scientists estimate there are about a quadrillion individual ants on Earth!

● What do ants look like?

Most ants are brown, rust, or black, but some are yellow, green, blue, or purple. The largest ant species can be more than 1 in. long, while the smallest is about $1/25^{th}$ of an in. long. Nonetheless, some ants can lift items 50 times their own weight.

● Where do ants live?

Ants live almost everywhere on land except for extremely cold areas. Some ants live in underground tunnels or build dirt mounds. Others live inside trees or inside certain plants. Some build nests using tree leaves. Army ants, however, do not have permanent nests; they walk in huge swarms, eating other insects they meet.

● What is life like in an ant colony?

Ant colonies may grow to have hundreds of thousands of ants. Inside their cities, worker ants do different jobs like clean tunnels, take care of babies, guard the city, and gather food. All worker ants are female; they build the nest, hunt for food, take care of the young, and fight predators.

Larger colonies have many queens whose main responsibility is to lay eggs. Males, whose only job is to mate with young ant queens, live in the colony nest only at certain times.

Ants, like other insects, also go through a metamorphosis. The larva is born without legs, and both the larva and pupa need to be fed and cared for by the ant colony before becoming adults.

Female ants take care of ant larva inside the nest.

Beatles

There's a good reason why 40 percent of the world's insects are beetles; they can **adapt** to many environments. The United States and Canada alone have 24,000 beetle species.

● What do beetles look like?

Beetles share some things in common with other insects; they have antennae, mouthparts, wings, and legs. They're characterized by their three sets of legs and their hard front wings called *elytra*, which cover the softer back wings it uses for flying.

● Where do beetles live?

Depending on the species, beetles can live in plants, tree bark, mud, tunnels, caves, water, decaying materials, and in other animals' nests and fur.

Beetle Facts

- Red milkweed beetles have four eyes.
- The number of spots a lady beetle (also known as a ladybug) has depends on its species, not its age.
- Some ladybugs have no spots, while others have stripes.

Beetles have antennae that are very different from those of other insects.

● What does a beetle eat?

Different beetles eat different things; some of these beetles are harmful and some are helpful. Colorado potato beetles can destroy entire crops of potatoes, and the elm bark, wood-boring, and long-horned beetles damage tree bark, fruit, leaves, roots, and stems. In contrast, ground beetles eat harmful gypsy moth caterpillars, while ladybugs eat the aphids and other insects that are harmful to plants. Dung and burying beetles also help clean up fields and wooded areas by eating decayed plant and animal waste.

The dung beetle may eat gross things, but it does its part to remove millions of tons of waste from the environment!

In northeastern states, ground beetles eat harmful gypsy moth caterpillars, which damage one million acres of forest each year.

Mammals

What kind of animal is warm-blooded, has hair or fur, and either four legs or two arms and two legs? Does all of this sound familiar? It should—it's a mammal, and you're a mammal, too!

Mammals, like amphibians, reptiles, and birds, have a back bone. Some mammals live in the ocean, others lay eggs, and some even fly. But that's where most of the similarities end. Unlike animals in the other groups, all mammals are warm-blooded and feed their babies with milk from their bodies—even if the babies hatched out of eggs!

The human life cycle includes being a baby, a child, an adolescent, a young adult, and an older adult.

Mammals are a very diverse group. Whales, apes, rats, cats, dogs, elephants, bats, and the egg-laying platypus are all mammals. But one thing all mammals, including humans, have in common is the mammal life cycle.

Most mammal young are born fully developed, and they drink milk from their mothers until they are able to eat solid food. Mammals also have a long period after birth during which they are completely dependent on their mothers. Once they grow and learn to hunt and protect themselves, young mammals may leave to hunt and live alone or to live with a mate and raise their young.

Whales, Dolphins, and Porpoises

Whales, dolphins, and porpoises are all large mammals that live in the sea. Although they spend their lives in water, they breathe using lungs, have babies, and feed those babies milk. Some whales even have a tiny bit of hair!

● What do whales look like?

A whale's body is much like a fish. The front limbs, also called flippers, are paddle-shaped. The end of the tail holds the fluke, or tail fins, which speed the whale through the water. Some species of whales also have a fin on their backs.

Whales also have a rubbery skin that covers a thick layer of fat called *blubber*. This blubber keeps the whale warm and provides energy for swimming and diving.

Whales breathe through blowholes, located on the top of the head. This, combined with the special structure of their lungs, allows whales to stay underwater for a long period of time.

Whale Facts

- Whales make sounds called songs, whistles, and clicks that can be heard for miles underwater.
- Whales have to be awake to breathe. Some scientists think that only half of a whale's brain sleeps at a time.

● What do dolphins and porpoises look like?

Most dolphins and porpoises have wide heads and sturdy, thick bodies that narrow toward their tails. They also have long flippers and a tall fin on their backs. Their bodies are usually gray, and their stomachs are white.

A dolphin has a beak and can grow to 12 ft. long. A porpoise is smaller, beakless, and usually only grows between 3–6 ft. in length.

● How do dolphins and porpoises have babies?

Female dolphins and porpoises usually give birth to one baby, or calf, at a time. When a dolphin is ready to have her calf, other females gather around the pregnant mother to help. Once the calf is born, other dolphins help the calf toward the surface to breathe. A newborn baby dolphin or porpoise is able to swim and breathe on its own within the first few minutes of life.

Compare a Dolphin and a Porpoise

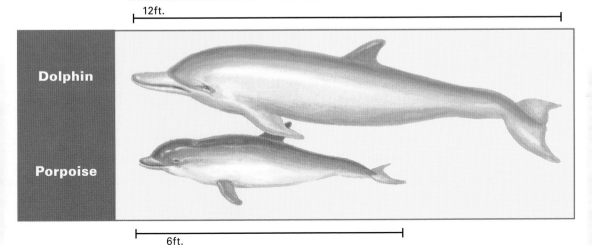

12ft.

Dolphin

Porpoise

6ft.

45

African Elephants

The African elephant is the biggest and strongest land animal living on Earth today and usually lives about 50–60 years in the wild. A large male can weigh anywhere from 8,000 to 15,000 lbs.

● What do elephants look like?

Elephants not only have huge bodies, they also have huge ears that they flap like fans to cool themselves down. This is important because their big bodies lose heat slowly and, unlike humans, elephants can't sweat to cool off.

Elephants also have long trunks that they use to smell, to feel along the ground, and to pick up objects. At the tip of their trunks they have one or two "fingers" which can pick up something as small as a peanut. By using their entire trunks, however, they can lift something as large as a tree.

Elephant Facts

- An elephant has only four teeth inside its mouth, but each tooth is huge, weighing more than a brick.
- African elephants usually have two extra front teeth called tusks. These tusks are made of ivory. The longest tusks measured 11.5 ft. long, and the heaviest ones weighed 260 lbs.

● How are elephants born and cared for?

Female elephants are pregnant for about two years, and when their babies are born, they may weigh up to 250 lbs! Elephants live in large groups of females who are all related. When a baby elephant is born, all of the members of the group are involved and will "babysit" the baby elephant while the mother eats. Baby elephants drink about three gallons of their mother's milk every day and put on weight very quickly—approximately 25–40 lbs. per month.

A baby elephant is often cared for by its aunts and sisters as well as its mother.

Rodents

Hear that scurrying and chewing? Is it a rat? A mouse? Rodents such as these make up the largest group of mammals—over 40 percent of mammals are rodents! Rodents are found on all continents except Antarctica, and they can live in all habitats except oceans. Their success in so many places is probably due to their small size, ability to breed quickly, and long front teeth that help them gnaw and eat many different kinds of food. Let's look at the kangaroo rat, a member of this large group, to learn more.

● What do kangaroo rats look like?

Kangaroo rats get their name from their large cheek pouches that they use to carry things and their large hind legs and feet that they use to hop like a kangaroo. These nocturnal rats weigh only 1–6 oz., grow 12–14 in. in length, and are known for their high-pitched, mouse-like sound.

Kangaroo Rats In North America

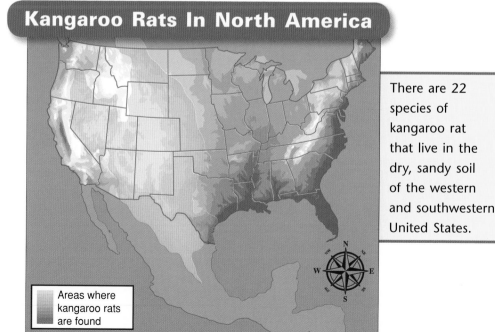

There are 22 species of kangaroo rat that live in the dry, sandy soil of the western and southwestern United States.

Areas where kangaroo rats are found

● What do kangaroo rats eat?

Like other rodents, kangaroo rats eat seeds, leaves, stems, insects, and grains. They often store food during weeks of very cold or very hot weather so they don't have to come out of their tunnels.

Because their bodies are designed to hold as much water as possible, kangaroo rats don't sweat or pant like other land mammals, nor do they need as much water. Their bodies are even able to change the seeds they've swallowed into a liquid.

● How are kangaroo rats born?

Female kangaroo rats build soft, grassy nests inside underground tunnels that also include dens for sleeping and eating. They generally give birth twice a year, with one to seven babies in each litter. Babies are born without hair, teeth, or the ability to see. They weigh less than a feather—1/16th of an oz.

A kangaroo rat's nest is in a maze of tunnels underground.

Rodent Facts

- Rodent teeth are constantly growing, so they have to gnaw to keep them from growing too long.
- Rodents, such as a giant beaver called *Castoroides,* existed in prehistoric times.

Felines

Do you or someone you know have a pet cat? Can you believe that this small, fluffy, purring creature belongs to the same group of animals as lions and tigers? They are all felines.

● What do felines look like?

Big or small, all felines are carnivores, and they are all built to be hunters. Along with slim, muscular bodies and powerful legs that allow them to run fast and leap great distances, felines have a set of tools that allow them to be super predators, which means that they are very successful at killing any prey smaller than themselves.

These tools include special eyes, claws, and teeth. Since felines are nocturnal, they have special eyes that allow them to see well at night. Felines also have very sharp claws that are good for ripping and tearing. These claws can also be retracted, or pulled back into their paws when they are not needed. Finally, felines have very four long sharp teeth on the top and bottom of their mouths that allow them to pierce and tear the skin off other animals.

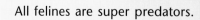

All felines are super predators.

● How do felines hunt?

Most felines surprise their prey, rushing up and leaping to use their body size and strength to knock prey off balance. Once the prey is knocked down, the feline will usually bite the back of the animal's neck to kill it.

Some felines have interesting ways of hunting their prey. The fishing cat pats the water to make it seem like an insect has landed, causing hungry fish to come to the surface. The cat then dives right in and grabs the fish. Geoffrey's cat, found in the southern areas of South America, walks upside down on tree branches and hangs by its back feet. This allows it to catch prey high up in trees.

Geoffrey's cat

fishing cats

Felines have about a dozen whiskers that help them get around. Their whiskers are super sensitive and can detect even small vibrations in the air.

Canines

Scientists may not agree on when exactly the first dog, or canine, was domesticated, or trained to live with humans, but few will argue that dogs and humans have a special relationship. When playing a game of fetch with your family's pet, however, you might stop and think about how the same loyalty helps dogs in the wild as they hunt and live in packs.

● What do canines look like?

Because they, too, are hunters, canines share many characteristics with felines. Wild canines, such as wolves and dingos, have long legs and bodies, sharp claws, and sharp teeth. Their claws are not used for ripping, as a feline's are, however, but to allow them to run fast. Also, unlike cats, which rely on their nocturnal eyesight, canines rely strongly on their sense of smell as they hunt, so they have long snouts.

The same loyalty that a pet dog shows humans helps dogs survive in the wild.

● How do canines live together?

Many groups of wild dogs, such as wolves, live and hunt in packs of seven to twenty dogs. These packs have an alpha male and an alpha female who have more freedom and power in the pack. The alpha male and female are usually the only pair in the pack to give birth to and raise puppies.

Wolves have developed certain behaviors not only to show their position in their pack, but to share emotions, such as anger, fear, and happiness, with other pack members. The lower dogs stay in the pack for many reasons, including hunting success and protection. Many packs also take care of their sick and older members.

Wolves have a very clear social order.

Conclusion

Every animal lives through a cycle that includes its birth, growth, reproduction, and death. All animals need a place to live, food to eat, ways to stay safe, and the ability to reproduce for their species to survive. Other animals have established strong communities to make sure they stay safe and well-fed.

Now that you've learned about some of the biggest, oldest, most numerous, and, yes, even the strangest animals on Earth, you're ready to take a closer look at the animals in your own neighborhood. See what you can find out about their amazing creature features!

Glossary

adapt to change to fit a new environment

camouflage patterns or colors that allow an animal to not be seen in an environment

carnivorous a meat eater

characteristics special features that make something what it is

cold-blooded body temperatures that change when air temperature changes

diverse having a wide variety of something

embryo an early stage of an animal's life

incubate to sit on eggs and provide heat to help the eggs develop and hatch

metamorphosis a change in the form of an animal's body

migratory seasonal movement from one place to another

nocturnal a night creature

predator an animal that eats other animals

prey an animal that is hunted for food

reproduce to make or produce again

species groups of life forms that have certain things in common

toxic poisonous

unique special

Index